nature & science

Developed by Macmillan Educational Company
Written by Joan Bielitz and Marilyn LaPenta
Text illustrated by Patricia Schories
Cover illustrated by Patrick Girouard

Newbridge Educational Programs

TABLE OF CONTENTS

TABLE OF CONTENTS
Continued

Use these activities to teach children what plants need in order to grow.

PLANT CARE

You need: four potted plants (grape or Swedish ivy, spider plants, philodendrons)
masking tape
marker
water
closet

Experiment #1

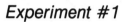

Steps:

1. Take two potted plants.

2. Use masking tape and a marker to label one potted plant "Watered Regularly" and the other "Not Watered Regularly."

3. Put them next to one another on a windowsill.

4. Water the plant labeled "Watered Regularly" every three days. Water the plant labeled "Not Watered Regularly" very rarely and very little.

5. After several weeks, ask children to describe what happened. Then have children draw a conclusion. (Plants need to be watered regularly to grow well.)

Experiment #2

Steps:

1. Take two potted plants.

2. With masking tape and a marker, label one potted plant "In Light" and the other "No Light."

3. Put the plant labeled "In Light" in a sunny window.

4. Place the other plant in a closet.

5. Water them both regularly.

6. After two weeks, ask children to describe what happened and then come to a conclusion. (Plants need light to grow.)

WINDOWSILL TERRARIUM

You need: 64-oz. plastic soda bottle
potting soil
small plants or seeds
scissors
water

Steps:

1. Remove the base from the soda bottle. (The bottle and base separate easily when pulled.)

2. Fill the base with potting soil.

3. Plant seeds or small plants in it.

4. With scissors, cut off the top third from the remainder of the bottle.

5. After watering the plants so that the soil is moist, place the remaining two-thirds of the bottle upside down over the plants.

6. Place the terrarium in a sunny spot and watch your plants grow!

Suggestion:

If you cut the bottle tops in advance for the children, they can prepare their own terrariums to give as presents for Mother's or Father's Day.

This experiment will help demonstrate that water is absorbed by plants and travels to all parts of a plant.

You need: tall, clear glass or jar
water
red food coloring
knife
celery stalk with leaves

Steps:

1. Fill a tall, clear glass or jar half-full with water.

2. Add a few drops of red food coloring and mix well.

3. Trim the bottom of a large stalk of celery. Leave the leaves on.

4. Put the celery stalk in the glass or jar. Leave overnight.

5. The next morning, observe what has happened. Let the children tell you where the water has gone. (The water has been absorbed into the celery stalk, tinting the stem and leaves red.)
Ask: Does the whole plant get water for food? (Yes.)

Follow-up Activity:

Take a celery stalk that has leaves. Trim the bottom. With a knife, make a slit up the middle of the celery stalk, stopping an inch below the leaves. Fill two tall, clear glasses or jars half-full with water. Add a few drops of food coloring to one glass or jar. Place several drops of a different food coloring in the second glass or jar. Mix the food coloring in each glass or jar well, and place the glasses next to each other. Put one-half of the celery stalk in one glass or jar, and the other half in the other glass or jar. Leave overnight. Observe what happens. (Each half of the celery stalk will have absorbed the colored water, and the two colors will have blended together as they moved up inside the stalk.)

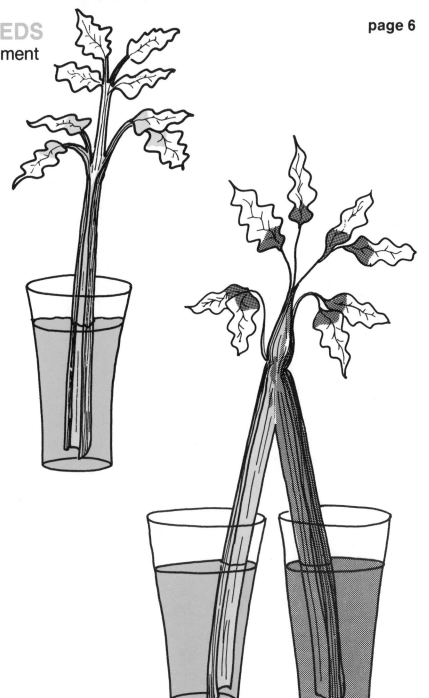

PARENT PLANTS
Growing Plants from Seeds

Let children observe plant growth through these activities and those described on page 8.

TRAVELING SEEDS

You need: dandelion blossom
covered with seeds

SPROUTING ALFALFA SEEDS

You need: alfalfa seeds (available
at health food stores)
water
wide-mouthed glass jar
(mayonnaise jars work well)
cheesecloth
rubber band
spoon
small plate

Steps:

1. Explain to children that most plants grow from seeds, which are produced after plants flower. Nuts are kinds of seeds. Some seeds are found inside fruits and vegetables (e.g., apples, watermelons, and cucumbers).

2. Blow on the dandelion seeds to show children how the wind helps carry these seeds to other places where they grow into plants. The dandelion seeds act like flying parachutes.

3. Ask children if they can think of other ways that seeds might travel. Some good answers:

   a. Squirrels or other animals may bury nuts and seeds.

   b. Prickly seeds (like burrs and thistles) catch on animals' fur.

   c. Birds carry berries and fruits containing seeds.

Steps:

1. Overnight, soak two tablespoons of alfalfa seeds in one-quarter cup of water. The next morning, drain the seeds and place them inside a large, wide-mouthed glass jar. Place cheesecloth over the mouth of the jar and secure it with a rubber band.

2. Then, through the cheesecloth, fill the jar with water, rinse the seeds, and drain the water from the jar.

3. Turn the jar upside down and use a spoon to prop open the mouth of the jar on a small plate so that air can reach the seeds. Store the jar, propped in this position, in a dark closet for two or three days.

4. Rinse the seeds once a day. Drain the seeds well so that they do not rot.

5. After the sprouts are about one-half inch long, transfer the jar to a sunny windowsill for another two or three days. Continue to rinse daily.

6. When the sprouts are green, they are ready to eat! Serve them on top of a garden salad or use them as a substitute for lettuce on sandwiches.

PARENT PLANTS
Growing Plants from Bulbs

BULBS

You need: large nail
two or three margarine tubs
pebbles
soil
crocus bulbs (can be purchased
in November and December from
a greenhouse)
water

Steps:

1. Explain to children that some plants grow from bulbs. The bulbs store food for the plants. The planted bulbs must spend several weeks in cold temperatures in order to grow well. During the cold period, shoots and roots develop inside the bulbs.

2. With a large nail, poke a hole in the bottom of each margarine tub. Cover the bottom of each tub with pebbles.

3. Then fill the tubs with soil.

4. In each container, plant three or four crocus bulbs, wide ends down, by just covering the tips with soil.

5. Water well. Always keep the soil moist.

6. Set the containers on a tray in a refrigerator or on a cold porch.

7. When the new shoots appear (in about 8–10 weeks) take the containers out and place them in a sunny window. Keep the bulbs at a cool temperature (50° to 60°). Flowers will appear in about a month.

Spring is just around the corner!

Variation:

Get a variety of different bulbs, such as tulip, hyacinth, and narcissus. Plant them in separate pots and label them before placing them in cold temperatures. After 8 to 10 weeks, remove them to a cool, sunny area and see how long each kind of bulb takes to flower. Then compare the blossoms.

SWEET-POTATO VINE

You need: sweet potato
toothpicks
wide-mouth glass jar, about 6" high
water

Steps:

1. Select a sweet potato with buds.

2. Insert several toothpicks around the middle of the sweet potato.

3. Place it in the jar with the wider end up. The toothpicks will hold the sweet potato in place.

4. Pour water into the jar so that the bottom portion of the sweet potato is covered. Add more water when necessary.

5. Place the jar in indirect sunlight. Watch for the roots to grow downward and the shoots to grow upward. Observe how long it takes for this to happen (about two weeks) and how long it takes for the sweet potato to grow foot-long vines (about six weeks).

6. Discuss other plants that grow on vines (cucumbers, squash, pumpkins, watermelons, grapes).

CUTTINGS

You need: half-pint milk containers
large nail
pebbles
soil
water
scissors
large coleus or English ivy plant

Optional: plastic wrap

Steps:

1. Pull open the tops of the milk containers and rinse them.

2. With a large nail, poke two or three holes in the bottom of each container for drainage.

3. Put several pebbles on the bottom of each container to cover the holes.

4. Add soil almost to the top of each container.

5. Water thoroughly.

6. Prepare cuttings by clipping small branches with five or six leaves from the plant. Cut the branches on a slant.

7. Make a deep hole in the soil, insert the stem of the cutting, and cover with soil.

8. Place the planted cuttings in indirect sunlight.

9. If desired, you can accelerate the root growth by loosely covering the plants with plastic wrap for a couple of weeks.

10. Ask: How will the cuttings get the food they need in order to grow, even though they don't yet have roots? (They have stored food in the stem and leaves. The leaves also continue to make food. This food nourishes tiny buds at the bottom of the stem and they develop into roots.)

Follow-up Activity:

Children can cover the milk containers with colored construction paper and draw designs on the paper. Children can then give their cuttings as presents to members of their families.

MARVELOUS MANGO

You need: mango
knife
8″ flowerpot
several stones, about ¾″ in diameter
potting soil
water

Steps:

1. Show children a mango. Let them touch it. Have them describe how it looks and feels.

2. Cut the mango into slices, and let children taste it.

3. Save the seed so that the class can grow a tropical mango tree.

4. Prepare the flowerpot by placing several stones on the bottom. Add enough potting soil to fill the pot.

5. To prepare the seed for planting, you must carefully slice open the shell of the mango's pit, removing the ripe seed. Plant the seed as soon as possible. Do not let it dry out. Place the seed under 2″ of soil, in a horizontal position.

6. Water the planted seed and place the flowerpot on a sunny windowsill. In about two weeks, the seed should sprout. The young mango plant has shiny, burgundy-colored leaves. As the plant grows, the children will notice that the leaves turn green.

Follow-up Activity:

Have children taste other tropical fruits, such as grapefruit, pomegranate, and papaya. Save the seeds, plant them, and compare the different plants.

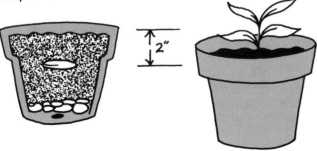

PERKY PINEAPPLE

You need: pineapple
several stones, about ¾″ in diameter
8″ flowerpot
potting soil
water
large, clear plastic bag
(large enough to cover the plant)
knife
ripe apple
rubber band or twist-tie

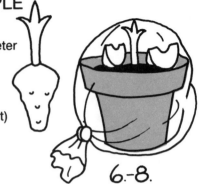

Steps:

1. Since it takes several weeks for a shoot to appear on the pineapple plant, you may wish to do this activity at the beginning of the school year.

2. Let children observe, touch, and taste a pineapple.

3. Twist off the leafy top of the pineapple, leaving about 2″ of the fruit below the leaves. Remove several lower leaves from the pineapple top. Let the pineapple top dry out for a couple of days before planting.

4. Place several stones on the bottom of the flowerpot for drainage.

5. Add enough soil to fill the pot.

6. Plant the pineapple top so that the exposed part of the stem is ½″ under the soil, and then water it.

7. Put the entire pot and plant inside a large, clear plastic bag.

8. Slice an apple into several wedges and place them inside the bag. Use a rubber band or twist-tie to close the bag and seal in the moisture. Place by a sunny window.

9. After three or four weeks, take the plant out of the plastic bag and discard the apple wedges. Water regularly, keeping the soil moist.

10. Watch for the shoot to grow out of the center of the plant (about two or three months later).

Note: As the apple ripens, it gives off a gas. This gas causes the pineapple plant to produce a bud, which will become a tiny pineapple. If this chemical process did not take place, it would take many years for the pineapple plant to produce fruit.

OAK TREE LIFE CYCLE
Sequence Story / Mobile

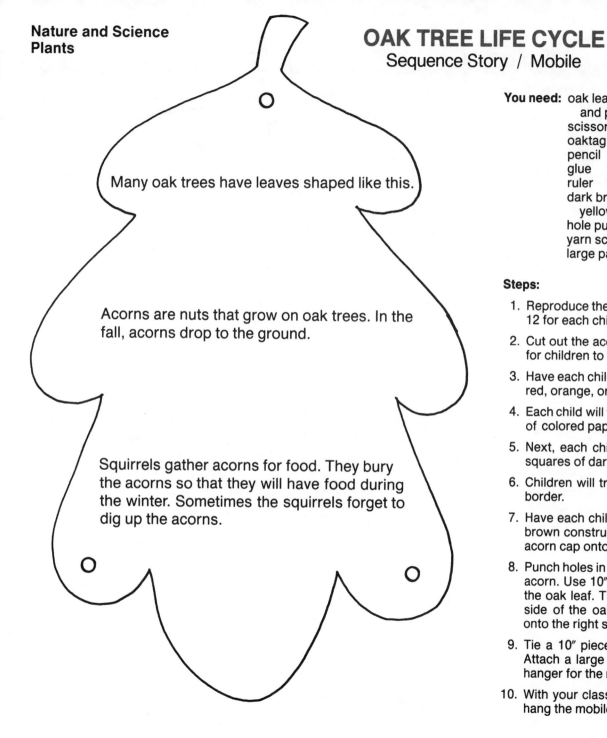

Many oak trees have leaves shaped like this.

Acorns are nuts that grow on oak trees. In the fall, acorns drop to the ground.

Squirrels gather acorns for food. They bury the acorns so that they will have food during the winter. Sometimes the squirrels forget to dig up the acorns.

You need: oak leaf and acorn patterns on this page
and page 12
scissors
oaktag
pencil
glue
ruler
dark brown, light brown, red, orange, and
yellow construction paper
hole puncher
yarn scraps
large paper clips

Steps:

1. Reproduce the oak leaf and acorn patterns on this page and page 12 for each child.

2. Cut out the acorn cap pattern and make several oaktag patterns for children to trace.

3. Have each child cut out the oak leaf and glue it onto a 9″ square of red, orange, or yellow construction paper.

4. Each child will then cut around the leaf shape, leaving a ½″ border of colored paper.

5. Next, each child will cut out the acorns and glue them onto 6″ squares of dark brown construction paper.

6. Children will trim around the edges of each acorn, leaving a ½″ border.

7. Have each child trace the acorn cap pattern two times onto light brown construction paper. Ask children to cut out and glue each acorn cap onto the top of each acorn.

8. Punch holes in the oak leaf where indicated, and in the top of each acorn. Use 10″ pieces of yarn to tie the acorns onto the sides of the oak leaf. The acorn numbered 1 should be tied onto the left side of the oak leaf, and the acorn numbered 2 should be tied onto the right side of the leaf.

9. Tie a 10″ piece of yarn through the hole in the top of the leaf. Attach a large paper clip to the free end of the yarn to make a hanger for the mobile.

10. With your class, read the story of how an oak tree grows. Then hang the mobiles in your classroom.

acorn cap

In the spring, a tiny seedling inside the acorn begins to grow. The seedling sprouts a root. As the root grows, it splits open the shell of the acorn. Then the root grows down into the soil. At the same time, the stem and new leaves begin to grow upward.

1

Buds appear on the stem. Shoots grow from these buds. The shoots grow and become branches. The stem thickens and becomes a trunk.

After many years of growing, the oak tree has a strong trunk. The branches are covered with many oak leaves. Acorns grow in bunches on the oak tree. In the fall, the acorns drop off the tree, and once again the squirrels gather them.

2

POPCORN

Ingredients: small amount of cooking oil
½ cup popcorn kernels

Optional: melted butter
salt

How to Make:

1. In a large saucepan or electric popcorn popper, pour a small amount of cooking oil to just cover the pan or popper's bottom.

2. Add a couple of popcorn kernels and cover the pan or popper. Heat the oil at medium-high temperature.

3. Listen carefully. When the kernels pop, add the rest of the popcorn to the oil.

4. Lower the heat and cover the pan or popper.

5. Shake the pan occasionally as the popcorn pops. When the popping stops, the popcorn is ready to serve.

6. Pour the popcorn into a large bowl. If desired, add melted butter and salt before serving.

7. While the popcorn is cooking, discuss why the kernels pop. (There is moisture inside the kernel. When it is heated, the moisture changes to steam. The steam presses against the kernel's covering until the kernel bursts.) Why didn't some of the kernels pop? (They may not have enough moisture inside, or they may not have been heated enough for the steam to burst the kernels open.)

POPCORN PLANTS

You need: 10-oz. clear plastic cups (one for each child)
water
paper towels
popcorn kernels
chart paper
dark marker
potting soil

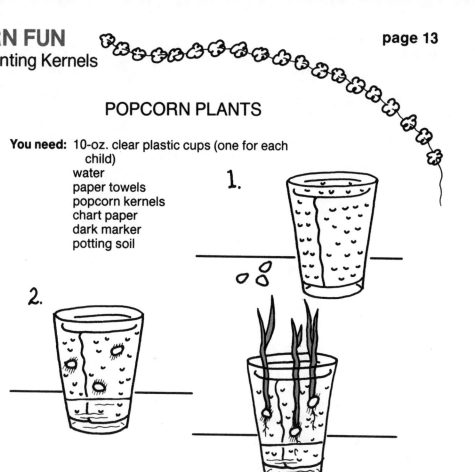

Steps:

1. Line the inside of each plastic cup with a moistened paper towel. The paper towels will stick to the sides of the cups.

2. Have each child place two or three popcorn kernels between the wet paper towel and the cup. Add 1″ of water to each cup so that the towel will remain wet.

3. Place the plastic cups near a sunny window.

4. On chart paper, keep a record of when the kernels begin to sprout (about four or five days after being placed in the cups).

5. Let children observe the popcorn sprouts' growth each day and record the changes with illustrations on the chart.

6. When each child's plants have developed several roots, they can be planted in potting soil in the same cup. Keep the soil moist, and place the plants where they will receive plenty of sunlight.

You need: ear of corn with the husks on
old newspapers
scissors
dried corn husks (collected in the fall
or purchased from a craft store)
ruler
aluminum pie pan
water
small rubber bands
string or yarn
fine-line markers
glue
dried peas, popcorn kernels, and beans
yarn scraps
fine rickrack or braiding

Steps:

1. Explain to children that, long ago, when American Indians grew corn for food, they used the corn husks to make dolls. Show children an ear of corn with the husks on. Explain that the husks form a protective covering for the kernels, or seeds. Pull off some of the husks to show the kernels. Then have children make their own corn husk dolls.

2. Cover your work area with old newspapers.

3. Trim the dried corn husks so that all the pieces are rectangular. For each child, you will need six 8″-long pieces and four 6″-long pieces.

4. Next, fill an aluminum pie pan with water. Dip the corn husks in the water for about 30 seconds. This will make them pliable.

5. Demonstrate to children how to gather the six 8″-long husks together, as shown. About 3″ from one end of the gathered husks, attach a small rubber band. See illustration.

6. To make the doll's head, have each child bend the ends of the corn husks down over the rubber band and secure with another rubber band. See illustration.

7. Next, ask each child to lay the four 6″-long husks on the table and tie the ends together with string or yarn. This is the arm piece.

8. Each child will then slide the arm piece between the free ends of the 8″ corn husks, just below the doll's neck, as shown. Tie with yarn below the arm piece to form the doll's waist.

9. To make a doll with a skirt, have the children fluff out the free ends of the corn husks. To make a doll with legs, ask the children to divide the free ends into two sections and then tie the end of each section with string, as shown. Let dry overnight.

10. When the dolls have dried, children will draw faces on them with fine-line markers. Then have children glue dried peas, popcorn kernels, and beans around the dolls' necks to make necklaces. Let children glue on yarn scraps to make hair. For headbands, children can glue on scraps of fine rickrack or braiding.

POTPOURRI PRESENTS
Scented Sachets

This activity introduces children to the different kinds of scents that plants give off.

You need: scissors
tape measure
1 yard of patterned fabric
pine needles
rubber bands
yarn scraps

Optional: pinking shears

Steps:

1. In advance, cut 4″ to 6″ squares of patterned fabric. Make one square for each child in your class. If desired, trim the edges of the squares with pinking shears.

2. Take a walk outside with your class in the late fall. Ask each child to collect a handful of fresh pine needles.

3. When you return to the classroom, give each child a fabric square. Ask children to turn their squares so that the wrong side faces up.

4. Each child then places his or her pine needles in the center of the square.

5. Instruct each child to carefully gather the four corners of the square, making a pouch for the pine needles. The child will hold the corners together while you or a classmate secures a rubber band tightly around the bundle.

6. Have children tie yarn scraps around their scented sachets to make decorative bows. These sachets make lovely holiday gifts.

Variations:

1. Use various spices, such as whole cloves, cinnamon sticks, or mint leaves, instead of pine needles.

2. Prepare the flower potpourri (see instructions on this page) and let children make floral-scented sachets.

3. Children may also make jars of flower potpourri. Have each child fill an empty baby-food jar with the flower mixture, then screw the jar's lid on tightly. Tie a ribbon around the jar's neck for decoration. Children may open the jars a little each day to let the delightful scent out into the room.

FLOWER POTPOURRI

You need: scented flower petals and leaves: rose, jasmine, violet, narcissus, honeysuckle, lilac, and so on
scrap paper
large bowl
spoon
flower oil (available at drugstores)
large screw-top jar

Optional: orrisroot (available at drugstores)

Steps:

1. Ask children to collect and bring in scented flower petals and leaves.

2. Lay the petals and leaves on scrap paper in a dry, airy place out of direct sunlight. Turn them over often, until they are thoroughly dry.

3. Place the dried petals and leaves in a large bowl. Mix gently with a spoon.

4. Add a few drops of flower oil for each pint of petals and leaves. Mix again.

5. Pour the flower petals and leaves into a large screw-top jar, and store for six to eight weeks. If desired, add a teaspoon of orrisroot for each pint of flowers before storing, to prolong the petals' scent.

Name_____

An insect has six legs.
Each insect has three body parts—a head, a thorax, and an abdomen.

At the right of the page, cut out the pictures of insects along the dotted lines. Then paste each picture in the blank box next to the matching picture.

beetle

ladybug

fly

bee

grasshopper

mosquito

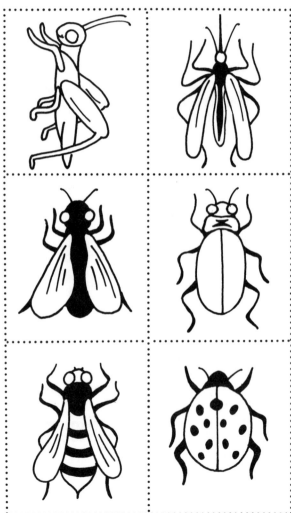

INSECT PUZZLES
Worksheet

Cut out the nine boxes below.
On a separate sheet of paper, piece the boxes together, in groups of three, to make three different insects. Then paste the pieces onto the paper and color each insect.

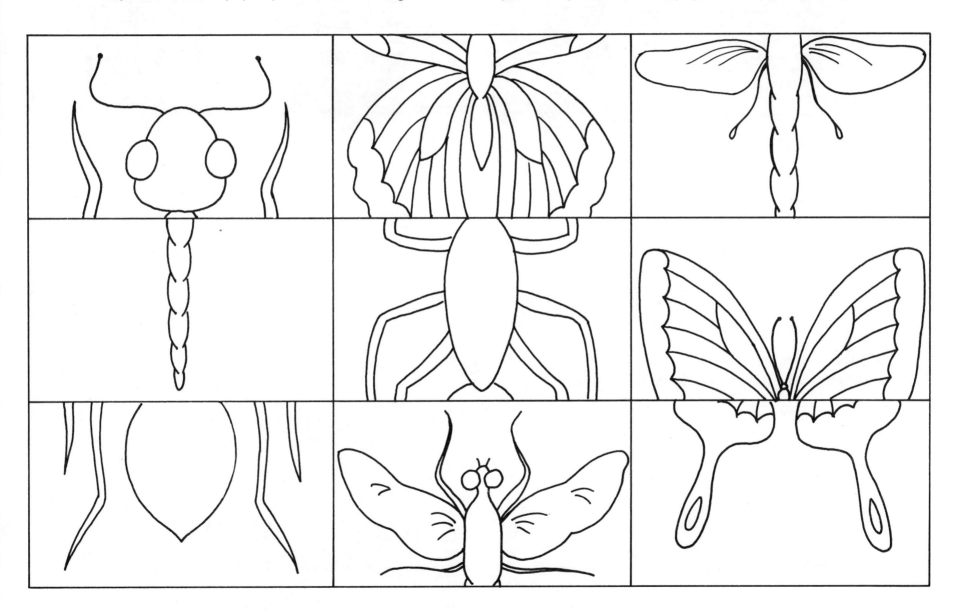

Use this activity to show children how worms help mix soil so that plants can grow well.

You need: damp soil
glass jar (approximately 1 quart)
sand
two or three worms
fresh leaves
cheesecloth
rubber band
tape
black paper

Steps:

1. Initiate a discussion on worms:

   Have you ever touched a worm? Picked one up?
   Do you like worms?
   What do people use them for?
   Why, do you think, are there worms in our soil?

   Children can learn the usefulness of worms by seeing what happens to soil in a jar when some worms are allowed to go to work in it.

2. First, put a 1½″ layer of damp soil in the bottom of a glass jar.

3. Add a 1½″ layer of sand, another layer of damp soil, and then a layer of sand.

4. Put two or three worms in the jar.

5. Place several fresh leaves in the jar for the worms to eat.

6. Stretch cheesecloth over the mouth of the jar and secure in place with a rubber band.

7. Tape black paper around the jar so that the worms think they are underground. Set the jar in a quiet corner for a few days.

8. Then, remove the black paper and let children look at the contents of the jar. Ask questions to help children draw conclusions.

   Are the layers of sand and soil the same as they were when the worms were first put into the jar? (No. The sand and soil are mixed together in places.)
   Why did the layers begin to get mixed together? (The worms dug tunnels through the layers and mixed them together.)

Explain that worms are helpful because they keep the soil broken up so that plants can grow roots easily. After children have observed the changes in the layers in the jar, release the worms outside in a shady place where the soil is loose.

You need: story on page 20
ladybug pattern
scissors
pencils
oaktag
8″ squares of black and red construction paper
hole puncher
glue
9″ × 12″ white construction paper
brass fasteners
black marker

Steps:

1. Make a copy of the story on page 20 for each child. Then reproduce the ladybug pattern on this page. Make several oaktag patterns for children to trace. To make patterns for the wings, cut out the circular part of the body and trace several times onto oaktag.

2. Have each child trace the ladybug body onto black construction paper and cut out.

3. With a hole puncher, each child will make two holes in the ladybug's head for the eyes.

4. Ask children to glue their ladybugs onto 9″ × 12″ pieces of white construction paper.

5. Each child will make the ladybug's wings by tracing the circular pattern onto red construction paper. Have each child cut out the red circle and fold it in half. Then unfold the circle and cut along the crease.

6. Next, have each child cut out the story and glue it onto the ladybug's body.

7. Show children how to overlap the tips of the two wings slightly. Have each child attach the wings to the ladybug by pushing a brass fastener through the overlapping wings and then through the ladybug, just behind its head, as shown.

8. With black markers, have children draw dots on the wings and add two antennae and six legs to the body.

9. Children can open the wings of their ladybugs to reveal the story.

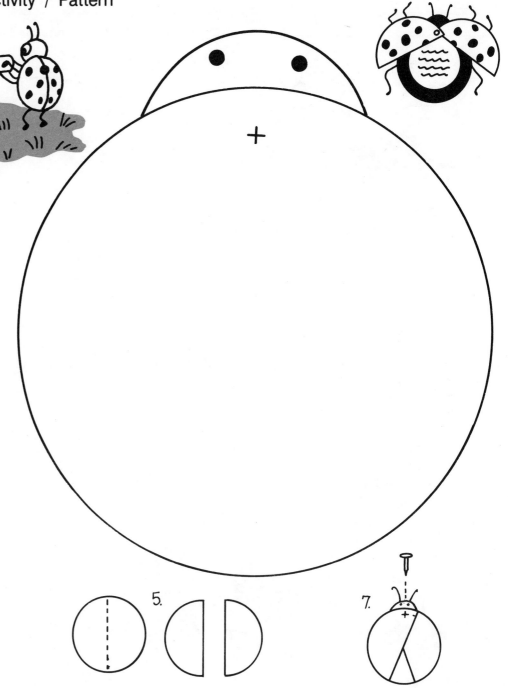

A ladybug is a kind of beetle. A ladybug's wings can be red, orange, yellow, or black. There are tiny spots on the wings. Female ladybugs lay tiny eggs. A few days later ladybug larvae, or babies, hatch. The larvae look like tiny worms. These larvae are helpful insects because they eat tiny insects that hurt plants. In three or four weeks, the larvae become adult ladybugs. In winter, ladybugs hibernate under stones or in houses.

HOW BEES MAKE HONEY
Make a Minibook

Color the four pictures on this page. Cut out the pictures and put them in order.
Then staple them together to make a minibook.

3. The bees fly back to the hive with the nectar.

4. They store the nectar in honeycomb cells
in the hive, where the nectar becomes honey.

1. Bees live together in a hive.

2. They gather nectar from flowers.

You need: fishtank or large glass fishbowl
gravel (can be purchased at a pet shop)
strainer
pails
large rock
large wide-mouth plastic jars with screw tops
a piece of screen to fit over the tank or
bowl's opening

Steps:

1. Prepare the fishbowl or tank by washing it with hot water. Do not use soap.

2. Rinse the gravel in a strainer until the water is clear.

3. Place the tank where it will get indirect sunlight.

4. From a nearby pond, bring in pails of water and several small plants.

5. Carefully pour the pond water into the tank, filling it about two-thirds full. Place a large rock in the tank. The top of the rock should protrude above the water. This will provide air-breathing animals with a place to sit.

6. After the water in the tank is clear, take your class on a trip to a pond.

7. Gather up various types of animals (water bugs, tadpoles, crayfish, and so on) in the strainer. Place them in the large plastic jars, screwing the tops on securely.

8. When you return to the classroom, transfer the pond animals and insects to the tank. Place a piece of screen over the tank to prevent the animals from escaping.

9. If you are lucky enough to have found tadpoles, your students will have the rewarding experience of watching them become frogs.

10. Add fresh pond water to the tank every two or three weeks. The fresh pond water will supply tiny animals and plants as food for your pond animals. Tadpoles can be fed lettuce, but once they become frogs it is difficult to find enough insects to feed them. Enjoy watching the young frogs for a few days. Then take a trip back to the pond and return them to their home.

Variation:

If it is not convenient to take a trip to a pond, go to a pet store and buy several guppies, other inexpensive fish, and aquatic plants for your classroom aquarium. Prepare your fishtank as described on this page. Fill the tank with tap water that has been aged in an open container for at least 24 hours. In time, your guppies may produce offspring, which are born live, rather than hatched from eggs.

SPIDERS ARE SPECIAL
Art Activity / Story

SUPER SPIDERS

You need: pictures of spiders and several insects
(bees, grasshoppers, flies, ants, and so on)
modeling clay
pre-cut 2″ lengths of pipe cleaner
(eight for each child)
peppercorns or popcorn kernels
worksheet on page 24
glue
colorful yarn scraps
crayons

Steps:

1. Display pictures of spiders and insects such as bees, grasshoppers, flies, and ants. Ask children to look closely at the pictures and describe the differences they see between the spiders and the insects. Ask: How many legs does each spider have? How many legs does each insect have? Do the spiders have antennae? Do the insects? How many body sections does each spider have? How many body sections does each insect have?

2. Then read children the "Facts About Spiders" paragraph on this page.

3. Give each child some modeling clay. Ask each child to make a model of a spider, showing the head and body.

4. Each child then takes eight lengths of pipe cleaner and inserts them into the spider shape to make the legs.

5. Have each child press eight peppercorns or popcorn kernels into the spider's head for the eyes.

6. Then make copies of the worksheet on page 24 for children to complete.

Follow-up Activity:

If possible, catch a spider and keep it in an insect cage (see instructions on page 30) for four or five days so that children can observe it.

FACTS ABOUT SPIDERS

There are many different kinds of spiders, of many different sizes and shapes. All spiders have eight legs. Most spiders have eight eyes. Spiders live wherever they can find food—in fields, woods, swamps, caves, and deserts. Spiders are helpful to us because they eat insects such as grasshoppers, which destroy crops, and mosquitoes. Many spiders spin webs to catch insects. Female spiders lay their eggs in silken egg sacs. Baby spiders hatch from the eggs.

SPIDERS ARE SPECIAL
Worksheet

Name_____

Trace over the spider's web with glue.
Then press pieces of yarn onto the glue.
Glue a piece of yarn on the paper to connect the spider to its web.
Color the spider.

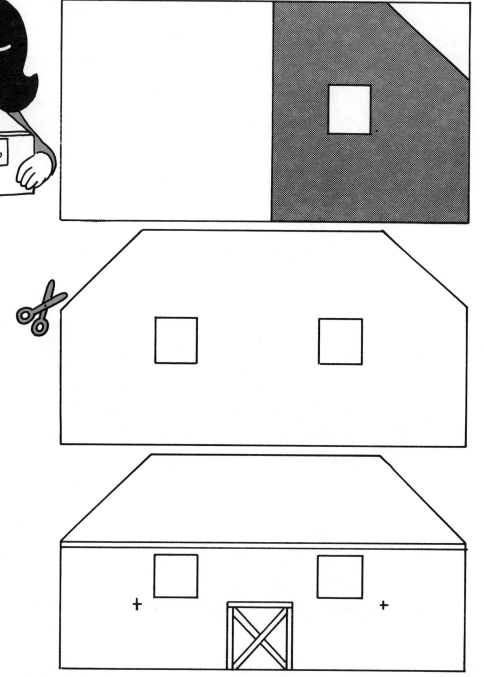

You need: barn pattern and picture wheel cutouts on
pages 26 and 27
scissors
glue
oaktag
9″ × 12″ red oaktag
pencil
9″ × 12″ white construction paper
two brass fasteners

Steps:

1. Reproduce the barn pattern and picture wheel cutouts on pages 26 and 27.

2. Cut out the picture wheels, mount them on oaktag, and cut out again.

3. Cut out the barn pattern and the window inside it. On a desk or table, place a 9″ × 12″ piece of red oaktag so that the long sides are at the top and bottom. Position the barn pattern over the right-hand side of the red oaktag, aligning it so that the lower right-hand corner of the pattern is even with the lower right-hand corner of the oaktag. See illustration. Trace the window and the diagonal side onto the oaktag. Then turn the pattern over and align it in a similar way on the left-hand side of the oaktag. Again, trace the window and the slanted side onto the oaktag.

4. Cut off the upper corners of the oaktag along the slanted lines. Then cut out the two windows.

5. From white construction paper, cut out several ¼″-wide strips. Glue them in place, as shown in the illustration, to outline the barn's door and roof.

6. Position the wheel showing the mother animals behind the left-hand window so that one picture is clearly visible. Push a brass fastener through the barn and the wheel's center, and open the fastener's tabs. Attach the wheel showing the baby animals behind the window on the right side of the barn.

7. Let children take turns turning the wheels and matching the mother animals shown in the left window with their babies shown in the right-hand window (duck–duckling, cow–calf, hen–chick, cat–kitten, dog–puppy, pig–piglet).

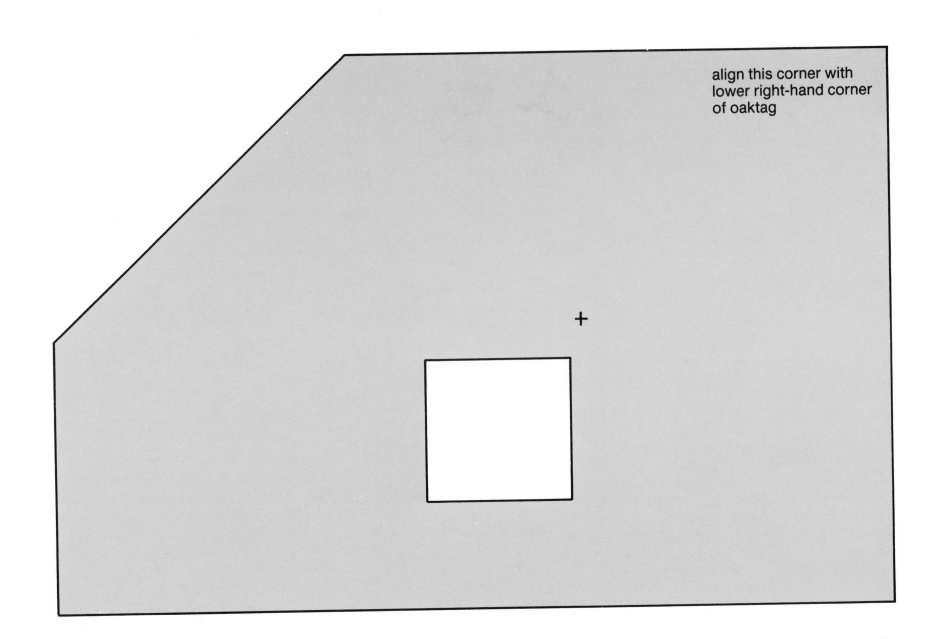

align this corner with
lower right-hand corner
of oaktag

MATCH MOTHER TO BABY
Picture Wheel Cutouts

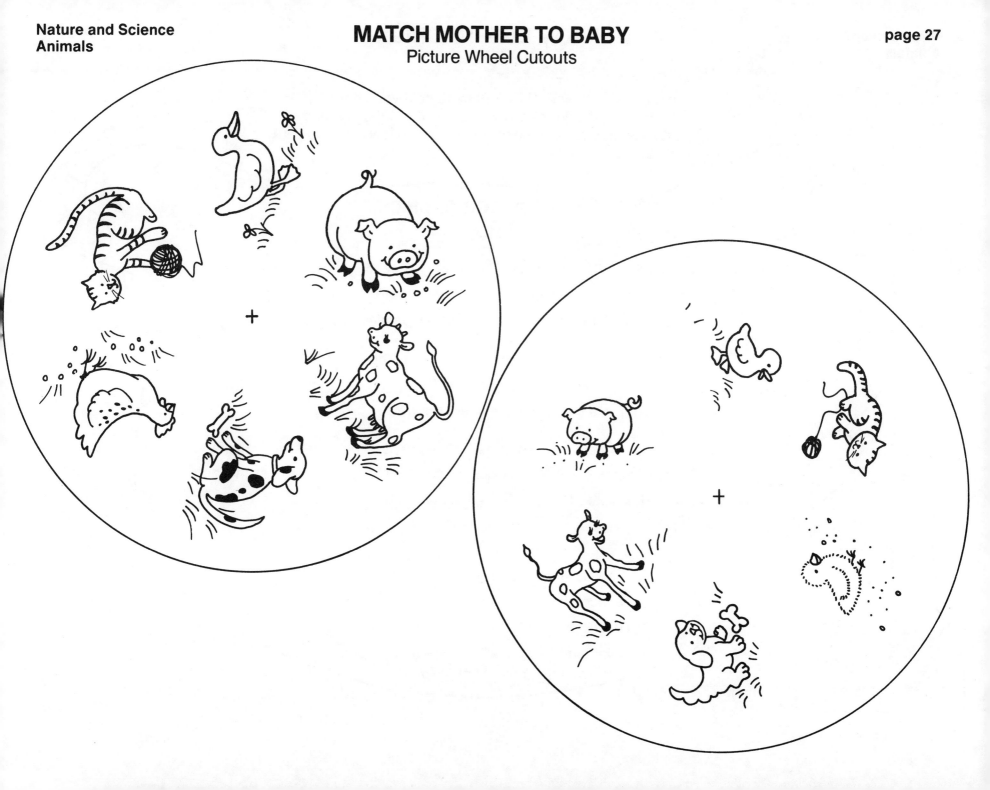

FROM EGG TO CHICK
Rebus Story

Read the story below. Use the key to help you figure out what the pictures in the story mean. Cut out the hen and paste it onto another piece of paper. Then follow the directions at the end of the story.

FROM EGG TO CHICK

A [hen] is a chick's mother. A [rooster] is a chick's father.

The mother [hen] lays one fertilized [egg] each day for a few days in a nest. Inside each [egg] a baby [chick] begins to grow. The mother [hen] sits on the [egg] [egg] for 21 days. She protects them and keeps them warm.

After 21 days each [egg] is ready to hatch. The [chick] cracks open the egg's shell. It may take hours for the [chick] to get out of the shell. When it finally crawls out, it is tired and its feathers are wet.

The [chick] rests for a while. Its feathers dry and become soft and fluffy.
The next day the [chick] is hungry and thirsty. It begins to eat mashed seeds and drink water. The [chick] grows until it becomes either a [hen] or a [rooster]

1. Draw seven [egg] [egg] under the mother [hen]
   Number them from 1 to 7.
2. Draw some straw around the eggs in the nest.
3. Color the face and tail feathers on the [hen]
   Lightly color her body.

KEY

[hen] = hen

[rooster] = rooster

[egg] = egg

[chick] = chick

FEED THE BIRDS
Make Your Own Bird Feeders

After making these bird feeders with your class, let children observe the different kinds of birds that come to the feeders. Children may also take the feeders home to attract birds in their own neighborhoods.

PINECONE FEEDERS

You need: large pinecones (one for each child)
12" pipe cleaners
large bowl
mixing spoon
16-oz. jar of peanut butter
2 cups birdseed
ice cream sticks or wooden tongue depressors

Steps:

1. Give each child a large pinecone and a pipe cleaner. Ask each child to wind one end of the pipe cleaner around the top of the pinecone and then bend the pipe cleaner's free end into a hook. See illustration.

2. In a large bowl, mix together the peanut butter and birdseed.

3. With an ice cream stick or tongue depressor, each child will press some of the peanut butter–birdseed mixture onto the scales of the pinecone.

4. Hang the children's pinecone feeders from tree branches. Cardinals, chickadees, and blue jays will enjoy these feeders. When necessary, add more peanut butter and birdseed to the pinecones.

Variation:

Cut out holiday shapes (bells, stars, pine trees) from heavy cardboard. Punch a hole at the top of each shape and tie a piece of heavy string or twine through it. Coat one side of the shape with a thin layer of peanut butter. Then press popped popcorn into the peanut butter. Hang the shapes from tree branches and watch the birds enjoy their holiday snacks.

SUET FEEDER

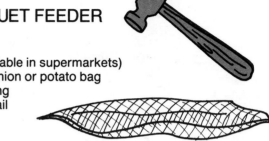

You need: beef suet (available in supermarkets)
plastic-mesh onion or potato bag
twist-tie or string
hammer and nail

Steps:

1. Place the suet in the plastic mesh bag. Use a twist-tie or piece of string to close the top of the bag.

2. Hammer a nail into a tree trunk and hang the bag of suet from the nail. This suet feeder will attract woodpeckers, titmice, crows, blue jays, and chickadees.

CROW'S CAFÉ

You need: soil
wide-mouthed quart glass jar
small plastic bottlecap (from a shampoo
or spice bottle)
water
twig and plant leaves or grass
insects to observe: moth, caterpillar, grasshopper,
cricket, ladybug, and so on
cheesecloth
rubber band

Steps:

1. Place a thin layer of soil on the bottom of the wide-mouthed quart glass jar.

2. Rinse a small bottlecap thoroughly and fill with water. Press it down into the soil.

3. Next, place a twig and several plant leaves or grass in the jar. Use grass or leaves that are found in the natural environment of the insect to be observed. (Collect the leaves or grass when you capture the insect for observation.)

4. Then place the insect inside the jar. Cover the mouth of the jar with cheesecloth, and secure it in place with a rubber band.

5. Let children observe the insect for several days. Then set the insect free.

Variation:

See if you can find a chrysalis or cocoon in the springtime. Place it inside the insect cage and wait for a butterfly or moth to emerge. Then release it outdoors.

THE ANT HILL

*Once I saw an ant hill, with no ants around
So I asked, "Little ants, where can you be found?"
Then before I knew it—one, two, three, four, five,
Five little ants crawled out, very much alive.
The five little ants looked all around for bread,
And found a piece to carry back, right upon their heads.
Then before I knew it—one, two, three, four, five,
All of them crawled right back, crawled right back inside.*

(Make fist with hand and put thumb in.)

(Lift each finger as you count.)

(Walk fingers around.)
(Move fingers backward—put two hands on head.)
(As you count, lower each finger and make a fist.)

ANT FARM

You need: glass bowl or jar
glass fishbowl
sand
loose soil
sugar
water
20 ants (from the same colony)
cheesecloth
rubber band
black construction paper
masking tape
bread crumbs

Steps:

1. Place a glass bowl or jar upside down in the center of the fishbowl.

2. Mix together sand and loose soil. Fill the space between the over-turned bowl or jar and the sides of the fishbowl with this sandy mixture. Leave the soil and sand loose so that the ants can dig easily.

3. Mix a small amount of sugar and water together and place several drops on the soil.

4. Put the ants in the fishbowl. Make sure that they are from the same colony so that they will work together rather than fight.

5. Cover the mouth of the fishbowl with cheesecloth, securing the cloth with a rubber band. This will prevent the ants from escaping.

6. Wind a large piece of black construction paper around the outside of the fishbowl, and tape in place. This will block out the light and make the ants think that they are underground.

7. Keep the fishbowl in a quiet area of the classroom at normal room temperature. Each day, open the cheesecloth lid and place a few drops of water on the soil. Once a week, feed the ants a few drops of sugar water or some bread crumbs.

8. In a few days, the ants will begin to build a nest, digging passages and making rooms in the sandy soil. Remove the black construction paper for a short time each day so that children can observe the ants at work.

You need: 12″ × 18″ white construction paper
9″ × 12″ construction paper of various colors
scissors
glue
odds and ends: buttons, felt scraps, yarn scraps,
  zigzag trim
fine-line markers
pencils

Steps:

1. Ask children to tell about their pets, including what kinds of pets they are, what the pets eat and how often they are fed, how they get exercise, what special kinds of homes they need, and so on.

2. Then have children make booklets illustrating their pets or the pets they would like to have. Give each child a 12″ × 18″ piece of white construction paper. Ask children to fold the papers in half to make 12″ × 9″ rectangles.

3. Give each child a 9″ × 12″ piece of colored construction paper. Have each child cut out a semicircle with a radius of about 5″ from the middle of one long side of the colored paper, as shown.

4. Children with four-legged pets (excluding turtles) can illustrate their booklets following steps 4 through 6. Children with two-legged pets or pet turtles can follow step 7. Have each child turn the white paper so that the folded edge is at the top. Each child will then glue the colored paper onto the folded white paper, with the cut-out section at the bottom. See illustration.

5. Ask children to make their pets' faces on the colored semicircles by gluing on buttons, felt scraps, yarn scraps, and zigzag trim. Some features can be drawn with fine-line markers.

6. Then have children glue their pets' heads onto the upper left-hand corners of their booklets.

7. Children with two-legged pets or turtles can decorate their semi-circles, as shown, before gluing them onto the fronts of their booklets.

8. Ask children to list the things their pets need inside their booklets. If a child does not have a pet, the child can write down the needs of a pet he or she would like to have. Assist children with spelling and grammar.

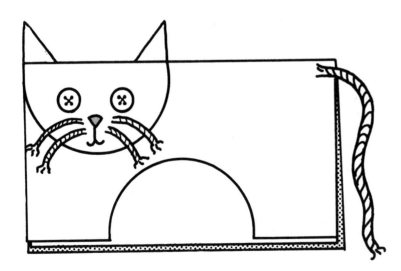

You need: worksheet on page 34
plastic tablecloth
large dishpan or baby bathtub
water
assortment of items illustrated at bottom of page 34:
   sponge, cork, wooden block, toy car, crayon, scissors,
   large paper clip, plastic straw
paste
scissors
crayons

Steps:

1. Explain to children that some objects float because they are less dense than water. Objects that are denser than water sink. Make one copy of the worksheet on page 34 for each child in your class.

2. Cover your worktable with a plastic tablecloth.

3. Fill a large dishpan or baby bathtub with water and place it on the table.

4. Place an assortment of items (illustrated at the bottom of page 34) on the table.

5. Nearby, on a desk or another table, place the paste, scissors, crayons, and worksheets.

6. In their free time, have children go to the table that has the container of water and put one item at a time into the water. Children will observe each object to see if it sinks or floats. After each object has been tested, each child will go to the nearby table and take a worksheet. Have children write their names on the papers. Ask children to cut out the pictures at the bottom of the page and paste each one under the appropriate heading. If the object sinks, paste its picture under the word *Sink,* where the boat is sinking. If the object floats, paste the picture under the word *Float,* where the boat is floating. If a child has forgotten whether an item sinks or floats, he or she may go back to the table and retest the object.

Variations:

1. Make this activity a guessing game. Ask children to predict whether an object will sink or float before testing it.

2. For additional experimentation, supply items that are not shown on the worksheet. These items may be drawn on the appropriate sections on the worksheet.

3. Let younger children experiment with the various objects, without completing the worksheet.

4. Make a chart of names and pictures of the items to be tested. This chart may be posted near the worktable. Older children may simply copy the word and draw the picture under a *Sink* or *Float* heading on separate pieces of paper.

SINK OR FLOAT?
Worksheet

Name_____

Cut out the pictures along the dotted lines.
Paste each one in the appropriate section.
Draw in any additional pictures in the correct section.

SINK

FLOAT

You need: clay
weeds, leaves, flowers

Optional: tempera paints
paintbrushes
shellac (available at hardware stores)

Steps:

1. Prepare clay (see recipe on this page) or use store-bought clay.

2. Take a walk outside with your class. Ask each child to collect a few leaves with large veins, some interesting weeds, or some flowers.

3. When you return to the classroom, give each child a lump of clay. Ask them to roll out the clay until it is flat and smooth.

4. While the children are rolling the clay, talk about fossils. Ask: Does anyone know what fossils are? How are they made? Explain that a fossil is a picture of a plant or animal that has been preserved in the earth for many years. After the plant or animal died, it sank into the mud and earth and made an impression, or pressed-down picture, of the way it looked. After many years, the mud dried and turned to stone. Now, when the stone is dug up, inside it we may find a picture of a plant or animal that existed many years ago.

5. Tell the children they are going to make their own fossils of the things they found on their walk.

6. When the clay is flat and smooth, have each child carefully press the leaves, weeds, or flowers into the clay. Children should press them in firmly with their palms.

7. Then have children pull the objects out slowly to reveal the lovely impressions.

8. Place each child's impressions in a safe place and let them sit for 24 hours.

9. If desired, children may paint or shellac their fossils.

Note: The fossils may also be baked in a pre-heated oven at 200° for two hours on a lightly greased cookie sheet. Cool in oven for two hours or until they are hard underneath.

Clay Recipe

Ingredients: 4 cups baking soda
2 cups cornstarch
2½ cups water

1. Over a low fire, mix the baking soda and cornstarch in a large saucepan. Add the water slowly to prevent lumping, and stir well.

2. Cook six minutes, or until the mixture has the consistency of mashed potatoes.

3. Spread on a cookie sheet to cool. Cover with a damp dish towel.

4. Knead for 10 minutes. If desired, add food coloring. Store in an airtight container. (Makes enough clay for about 20 clay fossils.)

Use this activity to introduce your class to the different types of soil and to show how the soil has settled over many years to form layers.

You need: plastic pails and shovels
sand, clay, gravel, topsoil
large glass jar with a lid
water

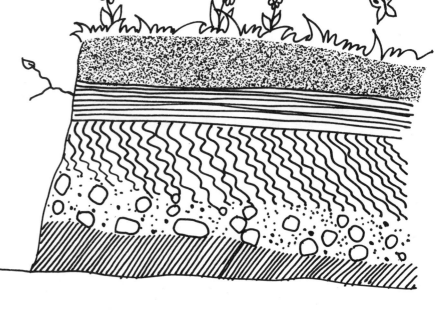

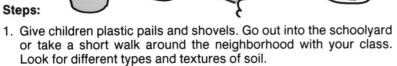

Steps:

1. Give children plastic pails and shovels. Go out into the schoolyard or take a short walk around the neighborhood with your class. Look for different types and textures of soil.

2. Have children collect some sand, clay, gravel, and topsoil. If all types are not available, bring some from home, or purchase from a greenhouse or nursery.

3. Fill a large glass jar halfway with the different types of soil, arranging them in layers.

4. Then fill the jar with water and screw the lid on tightly.

5. Ask children: What will happen when the jar is shaken? (The soil will get all mixed up.)

6. After receiving several responses, pass the jar around the room, giving each child a chance to shake it.

7. Then let the soil settle for about an hour.

8. Ask: What happened? (The soil settled in layers.) Why? (Some soils are heavier than others, and they sink to the bottom of the jar faster.)

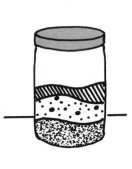

You need: model thermometers
(see instructions on page 38)
Fahrenheit thermometers (one oral and one outdoor)
bowl
several ice cubes
rubbing alcohol
water
saucepan
hot plate
scissors
glue

Steps:

1. Discuss with your class how thermometers are used. They measure the temperatures of many things. We use a thermometer to take a person's temperature to see if he or she has a fever. Thermometers can tell us the temperatures indoors and outdoors so that we can dress to be comfortable. We use thermometers when we cook so that we can be sure our food is prepared at the proper temperature before we eat it.

2. Then have children make the model thermometers, following the instructions on page 38.

3. After children have made their model thermometers, fill a bowl with several ice cubes. Place an outdoor thermometer in the bowl for a couple of minutes. Then let children observe where the red liquid inside the thermometer is. It should read 32°F, the point at which water freezes. Ask children to pull the strips on their model thermometers so that the top of the red section is even with the 32° mark.

4. Then set the outdoor thermometer on a desk or table in the room. After ten minutes, check the room's temperature. Have children move their strips to the appropriate mark on their model thermometers.

5. Next, dip the oral thermometer into rubbing alcohol and rinse well with cool water. Then take a child's temperature. Let children observe the liquid in the thermometer. It should read 98.6°F, which is the normal human temperature. Again, have children move their red strips to the correct mark on their model thermometers.

6. Fill a saucepan with a small amount of water. Heat the water in the pan on a hot plate. When the water is boiling, turn off the hot plate, and place the outdoor thermometer in the water. After a minute or so, remove the thermometer and let children see where the red liquid is. The thermometer should read 212°F, the point at which water boils. Children will then move their model thermometers' red strips to the 212°F mark.

7. After observing the different temperatures, children will cut out their temperature labels and glue them onto the left-hand sides of their model thermometers, aligning each label with the appropriate degree mark. (Have children write in the room temperature.)

Follow-up Activity:

Place an outdoor thermometer outside the classroom window. At the same time each day, check the temperature outside. Record the temperature daily on a wall chart.

Variation:

Use a Celsius thermometer to measure the temperatures of ice cubes, the classroom, a child, and boiling water, and compare the Celsius readings to the Fahrenheit readings.

Have children make these models of Fahrenheit thermometers before doing the temperature activity on page 37.

You need: thermometer pattern and labels on this page
scissors
glue
12″ × 6″ pieces of oaktag
1″ × 18″ strips of white construction paper
1″ × 12″ strips of red construction paper

3.

4.

5.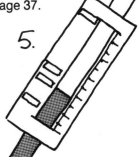

Steps:

1. For each child in your class, make a copy of the thermometer pattern and labels on this page.

2. Have each child cut out a thermometer on the outermost solid black lines and glue it onto the center of a 12″ × 6″ piece of oaktag.

3. Next, show children how to fold their thermometers in half on the long dotted line. Children will then cut slits at the top and bottom of the thermometers where the short dotted lines are. See illustration.

4. Give each child a white strip and a red strip of construction paper. Have each child glue the red strip onto one end of the white strip, as shown.

5. Then have each child thread the white end of the strip through the slit at the bottom of the thermometer and then through the top slit.

6. Have children save the temperature labels to use during the activity described on page 37.

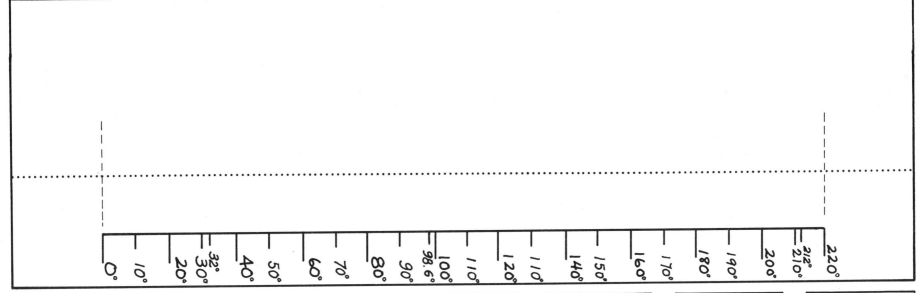

0° 10° 20° 30° 32° 40° 50° 60° 70° 80° 90° 98.6° 100° 110° 120° 110° 140° 150° 160° 170° 180° 190° 200° 210° 212° 220°

| Boiling 212° | Body Temperature 98.6° | Classroom _____ | Freezing 32° |

MAGNET MAGICIANS
Learning About Magnetic Force

This activity lets children observe the effects a magnet has on a variety of objects.

You need: bar or horseshoe magnet
paper
straight pins
large paper clip
plastic plate
block of wood
aluminum pie pan

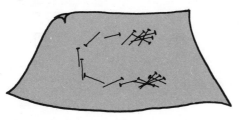

Steps:

1. After you have let children experiment with magnets, observing their ability to attract certain objects, use this activity with small groups of children. Lay a piece of paper on top of the magnet. Then drop straight pins over the paper. Ask children:

   What happened?
   Does a magnet have the same force at the center and at both ends?

2. Place a piece of paper on top of the magnet. Then, put a large paper clip on top of the paper. Move the magnet under the paper. Ask children: What happened? (The magnet attracted the paper clip through the paper.)

3. Let several children take turns trying to move the paper clip. Let them experiment, trying to move the paper clip on top of a plastic plate, a block of wood, an aluminum pie pan, and so on, to see what substances the magnetic force will pass through.

Follow-up Activities:

1. Have a child use a pencil to draw a path on a piece of paper, about 2″ wide. Ask the child to put a paper clip inside the path at one end of the paper. Holding a magnet under the paper, the child will try to move the paper clip along the path to the other end of the paper without going out of the lines. The child can have a race with a friend.

2. Tie a magnet to the end of a 2′ string. Place many objects (pencils, paper clips, bobby pins, crayons, pennies, and so on) in a bowl. Let children go fishing to see how many objects the magnet will pick up in one try.

Let pairs of children play this game at an activity center or when their work is done.
Children will observe the powers of magnets and improve their small motor skills.

You need: scissors
cardboard box, about 3' long and at least 1' wide
oaktag
two 12" rulers
tape
marker
two small magnets
glue or clay
two paper clips

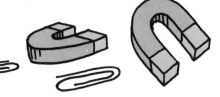

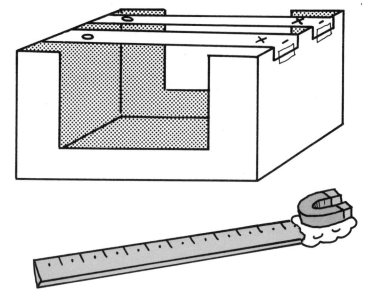

Steps:

1. Cut out a rectangle from each long side of the box. See illustration.

2. From oaktag, cut out two 2"-wide strips, 2" longer than the length of the box.

3. Tape the strips lengthwise over the top of the box, as shown. Space them a few inches apart. These are the racetracks.

4. With a marker, make an **X** at one end of each racetrack. This is the starting gate. Make an **O** at the other end of each track. This is the finish point.

5. Secure a magnet to one end of each ruler with glue or a small lump of clay.

6. Place a paper clip on each **X**.

7. Insert the ruler into the cutaway section. Holding the ruler so that the magnet is underneath the paper clip on the track, each player will try to move the paper clip to the other end of the track. If the ruler or magnet touches the track or the paper clip falls off, the child must put the paper clip on the **X** and start again.

8. The first child to get his or her paper clip to the **O**, the finish point, is the winner.

After making this art project, children can experiment with their helicopters to see how they fall through the air.

You need: helicopter pattern
scissors
pencils
oaktag
8½″ × 11″ paper

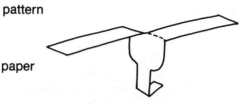

Steps:

1. Reproduce the helicopter pattern on this page. Cut out and trace several times onto oaktag. Then cut out the oaktag patterns.

2. Let the children trace the patterns onto pieces of 8½″ × 11″ paper and then cut them out.

3. Demonstrate to the children how to cut a vertical slit in the center of the **U,** as shown. Remind children to stop cutting about 1″ from the beginning of the stem.

4. Have each child bend one-half of the slit section forward and crease it.

5. Then ask each child to bend the other half of the slit section backward and crease it. These folded sections are the helicopter's propellers.

6. Next, have each child fold up the end of the stem about ½″ to make a rudder for the helicopter.

7. To fly their helicopters, have children stand on their chairs, holding the helicopters just below the propellers, with the propellers at the top. Children will drop their helicopters and watch them twirl to the floor.

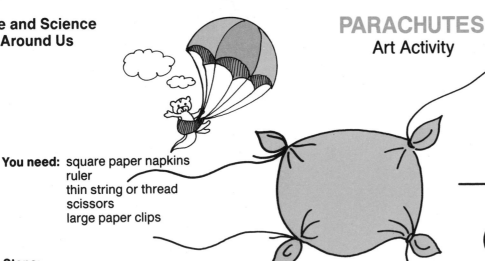

You need: square paper napkins
          ruler
          thin string or thread
          scissors
          large paper clips

Steps:

1. Give each child a square paper napkin, four 15″ strings, and a large paper clip.

2. Ask each child to unfold the napkin square on his or her desk.

3. Ask each child to bunch up one corner of the napkin and tie the end of one string around it. Have the children tie the other strings in the same way, one to each corner. Assist children if necessary.

4. Leaving the napkin on the desk, ask each child to gather up the four loose ends of the strings and tie them together in a knot (assist children if necessary). Leave about 2″ at the end of the strings, as shown.

5. Have each child tie the ends of the strings around the paper clip.

6. Each child will gently toss his or her parachute into the air and watch it glide to the ground.

7. Ask children: Why does the parachute glide slowly? (The parachute catches the air in it, which slows the parachute down.)

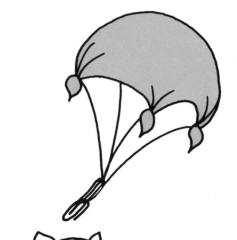

Variation:

Let children observe how objects of different shapes fall at different speeds. Give each child two pieces of typing paper. Let each child drop one paper and observe it as it falls to the ground. Then ask each child to crumple the other piece of paper and let it drop. Which one falls faster? Let children test other objects, such as a long, thin strip of paper, a paper folded into a small square, a paper folded into pleats and then opened, and a paper rolled into a cylinder.

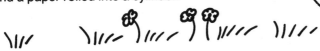

BALANCING BALLOONS
Experimenting with Air

Let children draw conclusions about air from the results of this simple experiment.

BALANCING BALLOONS

You need: two balloons of the same size
string
yardstick
sharp pencil

Steps:

1. Blow up two balloons equal in size. Knot the end of each balloon.

2. Tie string around the end of each balloon, and attach one balloon to each end of a yardstick.

3. Tie a 12″ string around the center of the yardstick. Hold the free end of the 12″ string and suspend the yardstick in the air.

4. Ask several children to hold the yardstick steady while you adjust the string to the center of the yardstick. The yardstick, which you are now supporting only by the 12″ center string, must balance horizontally.

5. Ask: What will happen if one balloon is popped?

6. Choose one child to come up and break one balloon with a sharp pencil.

7. Ask the following questions:

   What happened? (The yardstick tipped so that the end with the full balloon is lower than the end with the popped balloon.)
   Which balloon is heavier now? (The one filled with air.)
   How can you tell? (The yardstick is tipped so that the lighter end, the one with the broken balloon, is higher than the end with the full balloon.)
   Does air have weight? (Yes.)

AIR STRENGTH

You need: glass
water
squares of typing paper, slightly
larger than the rim of the glass
bowl

AIR MAGIC

You need: water
pitcher
funnel
thin-necked, transparent bottle
clay

Steps:

1. Fill a glass halfway with water.

2. Put a piece of typing paper over the top of the glass.

3. Hold the paper firmly over the rim, pressing over the edge of the glass.

4. Ask: What will happen when I turn the glass upside down and let go of the paper? Listen to several children's responses.

5. Then quickly turn the glass upside down over a bowl, holding the paper in place.

6. Carefully let go of the paper. (It will stay in place for a short time.) Then turn the glass upright again.

7. Ask: What keeps the paper in place?

8. Let children practice this experiment over the bowl.

9. Ask: Which is stronger, the water in the glass that is pushing down on the paper, or the air around the glass that is pushing up on the paper? Let the children draw their conclusions.

Steps:

1. Pour water from a pitcher through a funnel into a thin-necked, transparent bottle.

2. Let children observe the water flowing through the funnel into the bottle.

3. Then put clay around the neck of the bottle and the stem of the funnel. Seal the space between the bottle's rim and the funnel firmly. Let children assist.

4. Ask: What will happen when I try to pour more water into the bottle? Listen to several children's responses.

5. Then select a child to pour more water into the funnel.

6. Observe: What happened? (The water stayed in the funnel.) Why? (The air inside the bottle is pressing up and keeping the water from flowing into the bottle.)

Do the following experiments in the fall as part of a fire safety unit. When the conclusion is drawn from the experiment on the left-hand side of the page that a fire cannot burn without air, explain to the children that a small fire can be put out by smothering it. When children conclude from the experiment on the right-hand side of the page that warm air rises, they can be reminded to crawl low to safety if they are in a room that is on fire or filled with smoke, because the warmest air will be high in the room.

Can a fire burn without air?

You need: newspapers
knife
small pumpkin
spoon
candle
matches

Steps:

1. Cover a table with old newspapers.

2. Use a knife to cut off the top of a small pumpkin.

3. Clean out the inside of the pumpkin with a spoon. Let children help you.

4. Place a candle inside the pumpkin.

5. Light the candle.

6. Ask: When you put the top on the pumpkin, what will happen to the candle?

7. Ask a child to put the top on the pumpkin. Wait a few minutes.

8. Ask: What happened to the candle? (It went out.)

9. Then cut a face in the pumpkin.

10. Light the candle again. Ask: Now that there is a face on the pumpkin, what will happen to the candle when you put the top on the pumpkin?

11. Ask another child to put the top on the pumpkin.

12. Ask: What happened to the candle? (It remained lit.) Help children draw the conclusion that fire needs air to burn.

What happens when air is heated?

You need: plastic sandwich bag
glass jar
rubber band
pan
water
hot plate

Steps:

1. Put a plastic sandwich bag over the mouth of a glass jar. Secure the bag to the jar with a rubber band.

2. Put the jar in a pan filled with 2″ of water.

3. Place the pan on a hot plate. Heat slowly.

4. Let the children observe what happens when the air in the bottle is heated. (The bag is raised slightly.) Help them reach the conclusion that warm air rises.

5. Give some examples of other situations that demonstrate that hot air rises. For instance, an attic is usually hotter than the rest of the house; hot air is used to make hot-air balloons fly; the top floor of an apartment building is usually hotter than the other floors.

Does air have pressure?

You need: paper cups (one for each child)
clear plastic straws
water

Steps:

1. Discuss with the children the idea that air is around us everywhere.

2. Give each child a paper cup and a clear plastic straw. Fill the cups with water.

3. Ask: What is inside the straws? (Nothing, air, and so on.)

4. Tell each child to put the straw into the cup of water.

5. Ask: What is in the straw now? (Air and water.)
   What happens when you take the straw out of the water?
   (The water comes out of the straw.)
   Then, have children remove their straws from the water.

6. Next, instruct children to put their straws back into the water. Have each child put a finger over the top of the straw, so that they don't let any more air in.

7. Tell the children to take the straws out of the water.
   Ask: What happens? (The water stays inside the straw.)

8. Ask: What will happen when you take your finger off the straw?

9. Tell the children to remove their fingers from the straws.

10. Ask: What happened? (Air from outside the straw pressed down into the top of the straw and pushed the water out.) Let children draw their own conclusions, with guidance.

How strong is air pressure?

You need: narrow-mouthed glass container
shelled hard-boiled egg
scrap paper
matchbook

Steps:

1. Use this experiment only after you have done the pumpkin-and-candle experiment on page 45. Gather the children in a group around a table. Have on hand a narrow-mouthed glass container (such as a milk bottle or cruet), a shelled hard-boiled egg, scrap paper, and a matchbook.

2. Ask the children to recall what happened to the burning candle inside the closed pumpkin (page 45). (Fire used up air.)

3. Tell them you are now going to show them just how strong air pressure is.

4. Ask: What is inside the bottle? (Air.)
   What is pushing outside the bottle? (Air.)

5. Tell them you are now going to use up some of the air inside the bottle by dropping some burning paper into the glass container. Ignite a piece of scrap paper and drop it into the bottle.

6. Set the wide end of a shelled hard-boiled egg over the bottle's opening.

7. Say: Watch what happens to the egg after the burning paper uses up the air inside the bottle. (The air outside the bottle pushes the egg into the bottle!)

TASTY PUMPKIN TREATS
Recipes

Let children help measure and mix the ingredients in the following recipes.
Have children observe the changes in the appearance of the mixture during the preparations.

PUMPKIN PANCAKES

Ingredients: 4 cups pancake mix
2 eggs
3 cups milk
1 cup cooked pumpkin
   (canned or fresh)
1 teaspoon cinnamon
butter
maple syrup or honey

How to Make:

1. Mix the ingredients thoroughly in a large bowl. Let children assist.

2. Pour small amounts of the batter onto a hot, lightly greased griddle or frying pan over medium-high heat.

3. When bubbles form on the pancakes and the edges begin to brown, flip the pancakes.

4. Cook a minute or more, until brown.

5. Serve with butter, maple syrup, or a little bit of honey. (Makes about forty 4″ pumpkin pancakes.)

PUMPKIN SNACK SQUARES

Ingredients: 1 cup presifted flour
1 cup firmly packed brown sugar
1 teaspoon baking powder
1 teaspoon cinnamon
⅔ cup cooked pumpkin
   (canned or fresh)
½ cup margarine
2 beaten eggs
1 cup chopped nuts

How to Make:

1. Preheat oven to 350°. Mix the first four ingredients in a large bowl.

2. Add the next three ingredients. Beat until smooth.

3. Stir in the chopped nuts.

4. Then pour the mixture into a greased and floured 9″ × 13″ × 2″ baking pan.

5. Bake for 30 minutes.

6. Cool and cut into squares. (Makes about thirty 1¾″ × 2¼″ snack squares.)

PUMPKIN COOLER

Ingredients (per serving): 1 scoop vanilla ice cream
1 heaping tablespoon
   cooked pumpkin
   (canned or fresh)
½ cup milk
dash cinnamon

How to Make:

1. Let each child mix the vanilla ice cream, cooked pumpkin, milk, and cinnamon in a glass.

2. When the mixture is liquid, each child can sip this refreshing drink.

Where do the rain puddles go?

You need: large, wide-mouthed glass
water
masking tape
pen

Steps:

1. On a rainy day, put a large, empty, wide-mouthed glass outside your classroom window.

2. When the rain stops, put a 2″ strip of masking tape on the glass so that the top edge of the tape is even with the water level.

3. With a pen, write the name of the weekday on the tape.

4. Put the glass outside your window again. This time, make sure the glass is in a protected area, so that if it rains again, no more rain can get into the glass.

5. Check the water level each day. Record the water level daily by putting a strip of masking tape on the glass at the new water level. Write the name of the day on the tape each time.

6. Observe: How long did it take the water to disappear from the glass? (Introduce the word *evaporate* as another word for *disappear*.) Where did the water go? (It evaporated into the air.)

Variation:

On each strip of tape, write a description of that day's weather: sunny, cloudy, and so on. Let the children draw conclusions as to which kinds of weather make water evaporate faster.

Follow-up Activities:

1. After doing this observation activity, perform the rain and dew experiments described on page 49.

2. Try to make the water evaporate faster. Draw a line down the middle of a small chalkboard. With a sponge, wet each side equally. Ask a child to come up and wave a hand-held fan or a piece of oaktag to make the water on one side of the chalkboard evaporate faster than the water on the other side. Or take the chalkboard outside. After wetting it, put half in the sun and half in the shade. Observe: Wind and heat make water evaporate faster.

IT'S RAINING INSIDE
Simple Experiments

What makes it rain?

You need: box of seedlings or small plants
hot plate
metal tray, about 9″ × 13″
blocks or boxes
ice
water
teakettle

Steps:

1. Place the box of seedlings or small plants on a table. Explain to the class that this represents the earth. Next to the seedlings, set up the hot plate.

2. Place a metal tray, about 9″ × 13″, about two feet above the plants. Use stacks of blocks or boxes to support the tray.

3. Cover the tray with pieces of cracked ice. Tell the class that this represents the cold air above the earth.

4. Put water in the teakettle, and place it on the hot plate. The kettle's spout should point between the seedlings and the tray of ice.

5. Heat the water in the teakettle until it steams. Tell the class that the steam represents the warm air, which contains small particles of water, that rises from the earth.

6. Observe what happens when the warm air from the earth reaches the cold air in the atmosphere. (Drops of water will form on the underside of the tray and then fall, like rain, onto the seedlings or plants.)

What makes dew?

You need: ice cubes
metal bowl or container

Steps:

1. Do this experiment on a warm spring day. Put several ice cubes in a metal bowl or container.

2. Wait ten minutes.

3. Observe: When the warm air touches the cold bowl, some of the water in the air turns into water drops, or dew.

4. Have children look outside in the morning. Ask them to observe what happens when the warm air touches the cold ground. (Dew is formed.)

SNOWFLAKE STUDY

You need: 6″ squares of brightly colored felt
(one for each child)

Optional: magnifying glasses

SNIPPED-OUT SNOWFLAKES

You need: thin typing paper, cut into 8″ squares
scissors

FOLD   FOLD

CUT

Steps:

1. On a snowy day, have children dress warmly to go outside.

2. Give each child a square of colored felt.

3. Ask children to catch falling snowflakes on their pieces of felt, holding the felt horizontally with both hands.

4. As the snowflakes land on the felt, the children will be able to see the snowflakes' beautiful designs. Ask children if they can find two snowflakes that are exactly alike.

5. If small magnifying glasses are available, let children use them to look more closely at the intricate designs.

Steps:

1. Give each child an 8″ square of thin typing paper.

2. Ask each child to fold the square in half diagonally to make a triangle, as shown.

3. Have each child fold the triangle in half again to make a smaller triangle.

4. Each child will then snip out curved, square, and triangular shapes in each side of the triangle, being careful not to cut through to the other sides.

5. Have children unfold their triangles to reveal snowflake designs. Hang the children's snowflakes around the classroom.

SOLAR PRINTS
Art Activity

Plan this activity for a sunny day when the air is still.
Children will see the effects sunlight has on light-sensitive paper.

You need: blueprint or sunprint paper (can be obtained
from a graphic supply store)
folder
two aluminum trays, approximately 9″ × 12″
tablespoon and measuring cup
3% hydrogen peroxide (available at drugstores)
water
8″ × 10″ pieces of cardboard
variety of small objects to be printed:
    leaves, dried flowers, acorns, seashells,
    cookie cutters, nails, bolts, and so on
newspapers
glue
9″ × 12″ colored construction paper

Optional: 8″ × 10″ piece of clear, hard plastic
timer

Steps:

1. Keep the blueprint or sunprint paper covered in a folder until ready for use.

2. Prepare one aluminum tray with a fixer solution. To make the fixer solution, mix 1 tablespoon hydrogen peroxide with 1 cup water.

3. Put clear, cold water in the other aluminum tray.

4. Demonstrate to the class the procedure for making solar prints. Set up the equipment in a darkened corner of the room. Children may observe this procedure, but do not allow them to handle the fixer solution.

   a. On a piece of cardboard, arrange the objects to be printed.

   b. When you have made a pleasing design, remove the objects and place the blueprint or sunprint paper, blue side up, on the cardboard. Arrange the objects on the paper in the same design.

   c. If the objects are flat, a piece of clear, hard plastic can be placed on top of the objects to keep them in place.

   d. Expose the paper to sunlight by carefully carrying it outside or placing it in a sunny window. (Fluorescent lights will not affect the paper.) Expose the paper for two to five minutes, until the paper turns white.

   e. Remove the objects from the paper and quickly place the paper in the fixer solution for one minute. (Set a timer or ask children to count slowly to 60.) The images of the objects will appear light, and the parts of the paper that were exposed to sunlight will appear blue.

   f. Then rinse the paper in the cold-water tray for one minute.

   g. Lay the solar print on a piece of newspaper to dry.

   h. Change the fixer solution frequently so that the solar prints are clear. Pour used fixer down the sink.

5. Let each child make an original solar print, using a variety of small objects. Completed solar prints can be mounted on colored construction paper.

SUNDIAL

You need: small amount of clay
pencil
9″ square of white cardboard
   or construction paper
fine-line marker

SHIFTING SHADOWS

You need: chalk

Steps:

1. Explain to children that, before clocks were invented, people used the sun to help them tell time. Tell children that the earth revolves like a top that is slowly turning. As the earth turns, the shadows created by the sunlight change, becoming different lengths.

2. To make a simple sundial, roll a small amount of clay into a ball.

3. Push the eraser end of a pencil into the clay so that the pencil is standing upright. Then press the clay into the center of a 9″ square of white cardboard or construction paper.

4. Place the cardboard or construction paper next to a sunny window.

5. Every hour on the hour, have the class observe how the pencil's shadow moves and changes in length. With a fine-line marker, indicate the position of the shadow on the paper each time.

Steps:

1. On a sunny morning, go outside with your class.

2. Find the shadow of a stationary object (fire hydrant, fence post, street sign, bush, and so on). Trace the object's shadow in chalk onto the blacktop or sidewalk.

3. At noon, outline the object's shadow again.

4. Trace the object's shadow a third time in the afternoon, before the children go home from school. Then discuss the changes in the shadow's shape with your class.

Variation:

Let children observe the changes in their own shadows. Divide the class into pairs of children, and give each couple a piece of chalk. Have the children choose their places on the playground. Each child will write his or her name on the playground in chalk. While one child stands on his or her name, the partner will trace the child's shadow. Then the partners will switch functions so that each child gets his or her shadow traced on the ground. Repeat this procedure three times during the day—in the morning, at noon, and in the afternoon, each time having the children stand in the same spots as before, while their shadows are retraced.

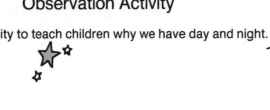

DAY AND NIGHT
Observation Activity

Use this activity to teach children why we have day and night.

You need: flashlight
worksheet on page 54
crayons
scissors
paste
6″ × 24″ strips of white construction paper

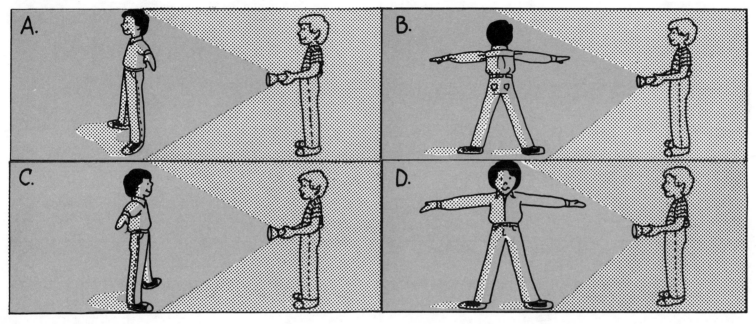

Steps:

1. Explain to the class that the earth is like a big ball. It turns all the time. We have day and night because the earth turns.

2. Choose one child to be the earth and another child to be the sun.

3. Give the sun a flashlight. Explain that the sun never moves. Ask the sun to stand still in one spot and turn on the flashlight.

4. Turn off the light in the room or pull down the window shades.

5. Let the child who is the earth stand so that his or her back is toward the light. Have that child hold both arms out to his or her sides. Say, "Turn to the right so that your right hand points to the light. The light is the sun. As you look sideways toward the flashlight, you begin to see the sun. This is the morning sunrise. Now turn your whole body to the right, staying in the same spot and keeping your arms out. Now you are facing the sun. This is day. Keep turning to the right. Your left hand is pointing to the light. Now look toward the light. This is the evening sunset. Keep turning. Now your back is toward the light. This is night. You have turned around once. You had sunrise, day, sunset, and night. When the earth turns around once, one whole day has gone by. The earth turns around once in a day."

6. Let the whole class revolve in front of the sun as described.

7. Reproduce the worksheet on page 54 for each child. Have children color the four scenes, cut them out, and paste them onto long strips of white construction paper.

DAY AND NIGHT
Worksheet

Color the four pictures below. Then cut them out and paste them in order, beginning with SUNRISE, onto a long strip of paper.

Name_____

SUNRISE

SUNSET

DAY

NIGHT

SUNRISE SNACKS
Recipes

Use these simple recipes to show children how changes in temperature affect food.

SUNRISE SALADS

Ingredients: 8-oz. can of sliced pineapple
1 cup water
3-oz. box of lime gelatin
small bowl
spoon
6″ paper plates (one for each child)
1 head of lettuce
knife
8 oz. of cheddar cheese (cut into
   approximately ¼″ × 2″ strips)
8 oz. of plain yogurt
forks

How to Make:

1. Drain the juice from the pineapple, keeping the slices in the can.

2. Let children observe as you mix one cup of boiling water with the powdered lime gelatin in a small bowl. As you stir the mixture, point out to children that the powder has been dissolved by the hot water.

3. Then pour the liquid gelatin into the can of sliced pineapple.

4. Tell children that you are going to refrigerate the can of pineapple overnight.

5. For a snack the next morning, give each child a paper plate with a lettuce leaf placed in the center.

6. Let children watch as you remove the gelatin from the can. (Run a little hot water over the can if necessary.) Ask children to recall what was put into the can the day before and describe what is in the can now. Explain that the cold temperature in the refrigerator made the gelatin become solid.

7. Slice between the pineapple rings, as shown, and then slice each ring in half.

8. Place a half-pineapple slice on each child's plate.

9. Let each child complete his or her sunrise salad using the cheese strips as the sun's rays and dabs of yogurt as clouds. (Makes 16 servings.)

CRANBERRY PINEAPPLE CRUSH

Ingredients: 46-oz. can of unsweetened
   pineapple juice
46-oz. jar of cranberry juice
blender, or hand egg-
   beater and mixing bowl
crushed ice or ice cubes

How to Make:

1. Pour half a can of pineapple juice and half a jar of cranberry juice into a blender or large mixing bowl.

2. If using a blender, add a small amount of crushed ice and beat for one minute, until the mixture becomes frothy.

3. If you are using a hand eggbeater to make this drink, add a few ice cubes before serving. (Makes about eight 4-oz. servings.)

Note: This makes a delicious frosty treat to accompany the sunrise salad.

Follow-up Activity:

After children have eaten their sunrise salads, ask them to think of other substances that are affected by changes in temperature (ice cubes, ice cream, chocolate, water, and so on).

COLORFUL RAINBOWS
Observation Activity / Art Activity

RAINBOW VIEW

RAINBOW MICE

You need: prism
18″ × 36″ white construction paper or larger piece of butcher paper
masking tape
thin watercolor paints (red, orange, yellow, green, blue, indigo, violet)
seven paintbrushes

You need: 12″ × 18″ white construction paper
watercolor paints (black, red, orange, yellow, green, blue, indigo, violet)
paintbrushes

Steps:

1. Discuss with your class how a rainbow is made. Explain that sunlight is made up of seven different colors of light: red, orange, yellow, green, blue, indigo, and violet. When sunlight passes through raindrops, the different colors of light are separated into bands. In order to see a rainbow, you must stand with the sun behind you and the raindrops in front of you.

2. Then show children a rainbow. Hold a prism by the classroom window on a very sunny day.

3. Observe the rainbow that is projected onto the floor.

4. Place an 18″ × 36″ piece of white construction paper in that spot and tape the corners in place to secure it. If necessary, use a larger piece of butcher paper.

5. Select seven children to paint the bands of color in the rainbow. Let the first child paint the red band of color in the rainbow with watercolor paints. Have the second child paint the orange band, overlapping it slightly with the red. The other five children in turn will paint the yellow, green, blue, indigo, and violet sections of the rainbow.

Variations:

1. Make a rainbow using a glass fishbowl filled with water. Hold the fishbowl next to a sunny window and see if you can project a rainbow onto a wall as the sunlight passes through the water in the fishbowl.

2. Children can try this simpler experiment at home with a garden hose. The child should stand with his or her back to the sun. The child then sets the hose's nozzle to make a fine spray. A beautiful rainbow should appear in the water drops.

Steps:

1. Give each child a 12″ × 18″ piece of white construction paper.

2. Ask each child to paint a black line from left to right across the bottom of the paper.

3. Still using the black paint, each child will paint a small semicircle, and right next to it, a large semicircle. See illustration.

4. On the small semicircle, each child will paint a mouse's face, with ears, an eye, nose, and whiskers. Then have each child paint a wiggly tail on the large semicircle.

5. To complete their rainbow mice, children will paint bands of the seven rainbow colors inside the large semicircles, beginning with red (in the outermost band) and ending with violet (in the innermost band).

LEAPIN' FROGS
Game

This game will help children learn that air can be a source of power.
It will also give them practice in measuring distances.

You need: frog cutout and lily pad pattern on page 58
scissors
pencil
green oaktag or construction paper
black marker
masking tape
12″ ruler
crayons
straight plastic straws
transparent tape
flexible (elbow) plastic straws
(slightly larger in diameter than
the straight straws)

Optional: frog stickers

Steps:

1. Reproduce the frog cutout on page 58 for each child.

2. Cut out the lily pad pattern and trace ten times onto green oaktag or construction paper. Then, cut out the ten lily pads.

3. To make a lily pad number line, number the lily pads from 0 to 9, using a black marker. With masking tape, attach the numbered lily pads so that their centers are 1′ apart. Children will use the number line to help measure how far their frogs leaped.

4. Ask children to color and cut out their frogs. Then, have each child write his or her name on the back of the frog. (If desired, frog stickers can be substituted for the frog cutouts.)

5. Cut straight plastic straws in half and give each child a half-straw.

6. Assist each child in folding over one end of the half-straw about ½″ and taping down the folded end. (See illustration.)

7. Have children tape their frogs onto the folded end of the half-straws, as shown.

8. Give each child a flexible plastic straw. Have each child insert the free end of the half-straw into the shorter section of the flexible straw. (See illustration.)

9. Each child, in turn, stands behind lily pad 0 and blows through the open end of the flexible straw to launch his or her frog on a giant leap.

10. Using the lily pad number line and a ruler, the child measures the distance in feet and inches that his or her frog leaped.

11. Make a grid on the chalkboard and have each child record the distance his or her frog leaped.

frog cutout

lily pad pattern

WONDERFUL WATER
Observation Activities

Let children draw conclusions about water from these experiments.

WATER POWER

You need: two bowls
water
tablespoon
salt
two raw, fresh eggs

Steps:

1. Fill each bowl with water.

2. Tell the children that you are going to do an experiment with salt water and fresh water. Then add four or five tablespoons of salt to one bowl and stir.

3. Ask: What will happen when I put an egg into the bowl of fresh water? Do this, and let children respond. Then repeat, using the other egg and the bowl of salt water.

4. Ask the following questions to encourage children to draw their own conclusions:

   What happened? (The egg in the salt water floated, and the egg in the fresh water sank.)
   Which type of water can hold up more weight? (Salt water is heavier than plain water and will hold up more weight.)

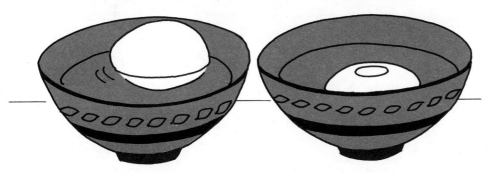

WATER MAGIC

You need: large glass jar
water
yarn or string
small glass baby-food jar
food coloring

Steps:

1. Fill the large jar two-thirds full with cold water.

2. Tie string or yarn around the top of the small jar.

3. Fill the small jar with hot water.

4. Add a few drops of food coloring to the small jar. Leave both of the jars open.

5. Ask: What will happen when I lower the jar of hot water into the jar of cold water? Proceed to do it.

6. Ask the following questions, and let children draw their own conclusions.

   What happened? (The hot water bubbled out of the small jar and rose to the top of the cold water.)
   What words could you use to describe what happened? (An explosion, a volcano erupting, and so on.)
   Did the hot water sink to the bottom or rise? (It rose to the top.)
   Which is lighter, hot water or cold water? (Hot water is lighter than cold water.)

WATER LENS
Homemade Magnifying Lens / Pattern

Make this simple magnifying lens for children to use when examining small objects.

You need: magnifying-glass pattern
scissors
pencil
heavy cardboard
clear plastic wrap
masking tape
warm water

Steps:

1. Reproduce the magnifying-glass pattern on this page.

2. Cut out and trace onto heavy cardboard.

3. Then cut out the cardboard magnifying glass.

4. Cover the glass's opening with clear plastic wrap. Tape the plastic wrap in place around the edges of the cardboard, letting the plastic sag a little across the opening.

5. Each child can use the water lens. Have the child place a small amount of warm water on the plastic wrap. He or she will hold the magnifying glass over an object of study (insect, plant, rock, shell, and so on), looking through the water to see the object's details.

Variation:

Let children experiment with the water lens, placing different amounts of water on the plastic to see how this affects the view of the object being observed. Keep the lens handy so that children can use it whenever they find something interesting to observe.

RAMBLING ROCKHOUNDS
Classification Activity / Art Activity

Use this activity to make children aware of the wide variety of textures, colors, and shapes found in rocks.

STONE SCULPTURE NOTE-HOLDERS

You need: water
paper towels
stones of various sizes and colors
glue
clip clothespins (one for each child)
shellac (available at hardware stores)
pencils
3″ × 5″ unlined index cards

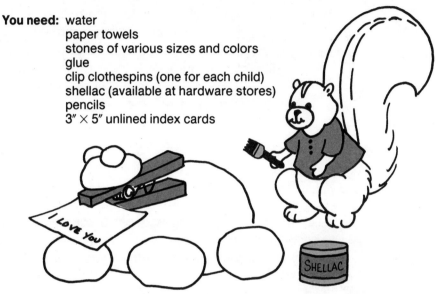

You need: brown-paper lunch bags

Steps:

1. Take your class on a walk outside. Ask each child to find several stones of different colors and shapes. Instruct each child to find a large stone (about 6″ in diameter) and many small stones.

2. Give each child a brown-paper lunch bag to hold his or her collection of stones.

3. When you return to the classroom, let children compare their stones, discussing the shapes, textures, and sizes.

4. Let each child sort his or her stone collection into groups by size, shape, and color.

5. Have children experiment with the rocks. Ask them to rub hard rocks against soft rocks and observe what happens. (Sand is formed.) Then, ask each child to try to write with a rock. Ask: Why do some rocks write and others don't? (When soft rocks are rubbed, tiny pieces crumble away and leave marks where the rocks were rubbed.)

6. Then, have children make the stone sculpture note-holders (instructions on this page).

Steps:

1. Before beginning this activity, have children wash and dry their collected stones.

2. Ask each child to glue a clip clothespin onto the largest stone that he or she found.

3. Then have each child glue the smaller stones onto the large stone and onto the top front section of the clothespin in a pleasing arrangement. See illustration.

4. Let the glue dry. Use shellac to give the stone sculptures a shiny finish.

5. Let children write messages in pencil on 3″ × 5″ unlined index cards and clip them onto their stone sculptures.

6. Children can take their stone sculpture note-holders home as presents to their parents.

With your class, discuss the animals, listed on this page and page 63.
These animals are commonly found in forests.
Then let children play the game described on page 64.

butterfly

Butterflies drink nectar, a sweet liquid produced by flowers. Female butterflies lay eggs. Caterpillars hatch from the eggs. When the caterpillar is fully grown, it spins a chrysalis. Inside the chrysalis, the caterpillar slowly changes into a butterfly. When the caterpillar is completely changed, a full-grown butterfly comes out of the chrysalis.

duck

Ducks have waterproof feathers and webbed feet that they use as paddles when they swim. They eat insects and water plants. Ducks in many parts of the world migrate to warmer places when the weather grows cold. They return to their homes when the weather becomes warmer.

fox

The *fox* has a bushy tail and a pointed snout. Foxes hunt mice, squirrels, birds, and other small animals. They have sharp senses of hearing and smell, and they usually hunt their food at night.

frog

A *frog* has long, strong hind legs that help it swim and leap. Frogs begin life as eggs. Tadpoles hatch from the eggs. Tadpoles have big heads and long tails. They can live only in water. In a few months, the tadpole grows legs, loses its tail, and becomes a frog. Frogs have sticky tongues that help them catch flies, worms, and spiders for food.

Opossums have grayish-white fur and long, thin tails. They live in trees, often hanging by their tails from the branches. Opossums have sharp teeth and claws. They search for food at night, and eat insects, eggs, and small animals such as mice.

opossum

The *owl* has a short, thick body with a ruff of feathers around its eyes. Many owls build their nests in hollow trees. They eat mice, squirrels, and rats. They have excellent eyesight and usually hunt at night. They have powerful feet, which they use to catch their food.

owl

Rabbits are small, furry animals with long ears. They live in shallow holes in the ground and eat green, leafy plants. In the winter, they eat the bark from trees and bushes. Their long, strong hind legs allow them to hop quickly.

rabbit

The *raccoon* has gray fur. Over its eyes is a black band of fur that looks like a mask. Its bushy tail has from five to seven black rings around it. Raccoons live both on the ground and in trees. They hunt at night and eat fish, frogs, fruits, and crayfish.

raccoon

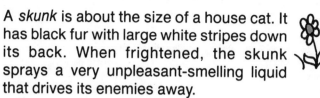

robin

The *robin* has a reddish-orange breast and brownish feathers on its wings and back. Robins build their nests of grass, twigs, roots, rags, and string. They use mud to hold the nests together. Robins eat fruits and earthworms.

skunk

A *skunk* is about the size of a house cat. It has black fur with large white stripes down its back. When frightened, the skunk sprays a very unpleasant-smelling liquid that drives its enemies away.

snail

A coiled, hard shell covers a *snail's* soft body. Land snails live in damp, shady areas, such as the undersides of logs or the edges of ponds. A snail crawls along on a strong, muscular foot. Many snails eat rotting plants.

swan

Swans are large water birds with white feathers and long, graceful necks. Swans eat worms, shellfish, and the seeds and roots of water plants. Swans that live in areas where winter is harsh migrate to warmer climates until spring. Swans make loud, trumpetlike noises.

snake

Snakes have no legs. They move by crawling. Several times a year, a snake grows a new skin and sheds its old skin. Snakes eat mice, lizards, and other animals. They swallow their food whole because their teeth are not good for chewing.

turtle

Turtles have hard shells that protect them. Most turtles can pull their heads, legs, and tails into their shells. Female turtles lay their eggs on land, burying them in holes dug in the ground. Turtles have no teeth, but they have beaks with sharp edges that they use to cut food. Turtles eat insects and plants, and sometimes fish, frogs, and snails.

squirrel

Squirrels live in trees. Their bushy tails help them keep their balance as they scamper along tree branches. Squirrels build nests of leaves and twigs in hollow tree trunks or on tree branches. Squirrels eat nuts, berries, seeds, and fruits. In the fall, they gather lots of food, which they store in holes in the ground, in tree trunks, or in their nests.

Woodpeckers use their strong, narrow bills to bore holes in trees. With their long, sticky tongues, they catch insects that live under the bark of trees. They also eat berries, fruits, and nuts. They make their homes in holes in trees.

woodpecker

After introducing the animals discussed on pages 62 and 63, invite your class to make their own forest animal story mat.

You need: large sheets of oaktag or mural paper
index cards
markers, crayons, or paints

Optional: clear plastic adhesive

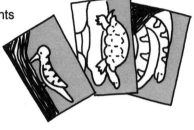

How to Prepare:

1. Divide the class into small groups. Explain that one group is going to create a story mat depicting a forest scene. The other groups will create animal cards.

2. Give the story-mat group a large sheet of oaktag or a length of mural paper, and instruct them to paint a forest scene, complete with trees, flowers, and a lake or stream.

3. While these children are working, pass out index cards to the other groups, and assign to each some of the animals from pages 62 and 63. Explain that on each card, they are to draw one of the animals. There are 16 animals in all. You might have students create two cards for each animal.

4. For sturdier cards, have students cover them with clear adhesive tape.

How to Use:

1. Let students use the story mat in small groups. Lay the mat on a table, with the animal cards beside it.

2. Tell students to choose an animal card and to place it on the mat where the animal lives. For example, a turtle would live in the lake. An owl or an opossum would live in a tree. Where would a butterfly spend most of its time? Or the frog?

3. Then challenge students to name each animal.

4. Now invite students to tell a story about their forest animals using the story mat and the animal cards. Might one animal visit another? Might the animals have a party? Might someone get lost here? Encourage the groups to share their forest stories with the rest of the class.

Variation:
If you created two cards for each animal, let students play "Concentration." Turn all the cards facedown. Children take turns turning the cards over two at a time. When a player turns over two cards of the same animal, he or she keeps the pair. The player with the most pairs wins. Students might also use the cards to group the animals by categories, such as animals with feathers, animals with fur, animals that swim, animals that fly, animals that run, and so on.